WHAT SOME HAVE SAID ABOU

G000096572

"These are poems to taste—ripe, suc
be lingered over for days and revisit
each sound and word, offering them to us on a gilt plate."

—PEGGY TABOR MILLIN, award winning author of *Women,
Writing, and Soul-Making: Creativity and the Sacred Feminine*

"Raphael Block is a poet who wears his heart on his sleeve. Like a
troubadour, he stands directly before you, without the armor of
irony or emotional detachment, or the high gloss of technical
formality, singing of love and loss and the natural world with a
rare emotional intimacy and an unblinking candor...This is the
essence of Block's poetry—the desire to use the raw materials of
his experiences and the gift of his five senses to make a genuine,
heart-centered connection with the reader. And, for this reader,
he succeeds."

—SARAH SAULSBURY, Director of the Occidental Community Choir

"A collection of sound quilts, *Spangling Darkness* weaves through
wonders of flora, fauna, motion and emotion. Using imagery both
haunting and reassuring, Raphael Block chooses his words with
precision, stones tossed into a vast pond, creating ripples, expanding
circles of spaciousness. And with each reading, more nuance,
deeper waves of understanding and connectivity."

—SHARON BARD, Author and coeditor of *Steeped in the World of Tea*

"Raphael Block's new collection *Spangling Darkness* illuminates
what often seems a chaotic world. He brings a penetrating
sweetness and wisdom to his observations of the world and the
human experience. This is an important contribution to the
world of poetry."

—LARRY ROBINSON, poet, producer of Rumi's Caravan, e-poem
a day, and former mayor of Sebastopol

SPANGLING DARKNESS

poems and songs by

RAPHAEL BLOCK

with original drawings by CLARE ALLEN

POETIC MATRIX PRESS

A link to the downloadable MP3 of Raphael Block
reciting all 44 poems in SPANGLING DARKNESS
is included with every purchase.
Copy into your browser:
www.poeticmatrix.com/raphael-block
and download the audio.

Poetic Matrix Press
www.poeticmatrix.com

PREFACE

It gives me great joy to share these windfalls. My hope is you may be nourished by some, touched by others.

My deepest thanks to my poetry teacher, Terry Ehret; Wellspring and Toppers Poetry groups for their feedback and support; Kathy Zurga and Nan Hopkin for reading this manuscript with a loving, critical eye; Kerry Yates for shaping and rehearsing four of the songs; Sarah Saulsbury for transcribing *Unbreakable Peace*, and for her choral composition, *When I Look at the Stars*.

I would like to acknowledge Nomi Rowe for publishing *Spring*, *Fallen Fruit*, and *Old and Delved* in her wonderful book, *In Celebration of Cecil Collins, Visionary Artist and Educator*, Foolscap Press, London (2008); Larry Robinson's E-Poem of the Day for sending out *The Kiss*, *When a Chill Sea Wind*, *Mute Millennial*, *Wired*, *Was it Writ* and *The Great Winter Wood Pellet Rush*; the Brian Kirven Show on KWMR for broadcasting *Between the Two Shores*, *The Inverness Ridge Fire*, and *Spring*; and J.Glenn Evans of KSER for featuring on PoetsWest #209 *The Kiss*, *Fallen Fruit*, *When I Look at the Stars*, *Soft Night*, *When a Chill Sea Wind*, *Old and Delved*, *The Conductor*, *The Great Winter Wood Pellet Rush*, and *Just When You Think It's Over*.

My publisher, John Peterson, has shown flexibility, perseverance, and great forbearance while bringing our shared vision to fruition. Thank you, John.

—Raphael Block

To my teachers, and Clare Allen, for their
generosity of spirit.

What price I pay by not living the self
worth living for?

Foreward

SPANGLING DARKNESS is a companion to Raphael Block's previous collection, *Songs from a Small Universe*. This is poetry that is in tune with being in the world and knowing how to live each day in concert with other living creatures, the trees and flowers, and with the family cat.

In a world that is increasingly homogenized, a world that seems to me to be arrogant and self-centered, we need to stop and listen to the earth breathing. As the poems in *Songs from a Small Universe* are like prayers, the poems in SPANGLING DARKNESS assume a sensuous delight that comes from close attention to the natural world and its rhythms. There is a wholeness and strength in these poems. As in *Songs from a Small Universe*, Raphael expresses the simplest and deepest of human feelings in the context of an awareness of being in the moment.

Now, while slowly wading | through tiredness and water | I settle. | Child's absorbed in homework | cat's content. | This is a good task. | I am doing well | to serve the moment. | What's more important?

Raphael's voice is a tool for sanity and survival in a world where hazards keep appearing on our path. This is a poet at home in the universe and the places where he has lived. He was born on a kibbutz in Israel and played on the hills of Haifa. Still a child when his family moved back to England, he learned English and was much influenced by the English language and the British climate. His life changed again when he met and married an American living in London. In 1993 they moved with their daughter to Northern California. After his wife died from cancer in 2002, he was left to care for and raise their daughter alone. He has worked with children of all ages for three decades. Living in an old apple orchard outside of Sebastopol, he considers himself richly blessed.

We see a measure of this serenity reflected in the poems through his insights and humor, his love for words and for music, and lively community life. These poems reveal his observations and artistic discipline based on the natural world and his life in the orchard. *With a whoop and a fling | blossoms she brings | singing, it's April | it's April | it's April.* The rich pencil drawings, by British artist Clare Allen, that accompany each of the four sections of poems further enhance and preserve the images and meanings of the lines.

Raphael was also an active member of the Occidental Community Choir. One of his poems, *When I Look at the Stars,* has been set to music by choir director, Sarah Saulsbury, and sung by the choir. It is included in the last section, *Songs.*

The poems in both *Songs from a Small Universe* and *SPANGLING DARKNESS* illuminate his love for life and engagement with the natural world and with the community. *SPANGLING DARKNESS* ignites the imagination for a new vision that allows the earth to mend. This is the gift of Raphael Block as a poet whose spirit resonates in our common humanity and binds us together.

—J. Glenn Evans, *founder and director of PoetsWest, is the author of two novels and four books of poetry, Window In The Sky, Seattle Poems, Buffalo Tracks, and Deadly Mistress.*

CONTENTS

Earth Dances

Songs

About the Author

Press Producers

SPANGLING DARKNESS

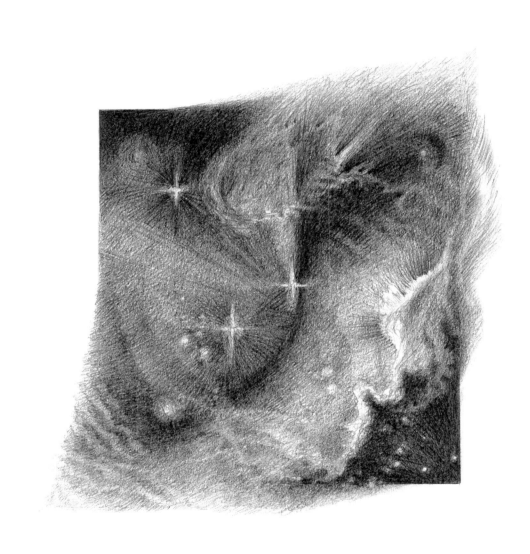

SPANGLING DARKNESS

למה שבקתני

Lamah shvaqtani?

"Why, oh why did You abandon me?"

In the silence of the tomb
he lay, or let's just say
his body did.

For that extreme,
when we can simply stand
no more, opens a door.

The cries of a lover betrayed
snapped cords
as he hurled himself into
the spangling darkness.

One caress
by the infinite —
balm enough for living!

A firm tugging, "There's
more to be done"
spun him back
into that body
in the silence of the tomb.

Two more nights and days —
how stretched he lay between
those countless moments

the stinging wounds
almost naught to the scarring
of his heart

those mocking jeers
still ringing in his ears
pale beside his realization
of our weaknesses and fears.

And when as warm, fresh
baked bread, he slid out
scented from that oven,
Magdalene gasped, squealing
in delight, "You've risen!"
followed by a long embrace.

He reentered this arena
a cross between
boxer and lover
punching, feinting
darting, weaving, dancing,
melting our denseness
and defenses.

CONCEALED

And then above, a squadron of some thirty long-beaks swoops speeding over the waves in a fluttering V before banking inland along the rich estero. In their wake the coastline takes me to two stationary figures watching a wave of tan, rounded forms, just a little darker than the sand, huddled on the spit. Most lie still as logs. Occasionally, a body undulates towards the water, rounded rear in the air. Others change positions among their close-knit clan. A few heads bob at sea. Periodically, on raised periscopic necks, three pairs of eyes swivel towards us. Quizzical? curious? checking for danger? those soft orbs from the mysterious depths. Walking back along the shore, washed up wood resembles seals, and from bleached trunks liquid irises peer at the odds and ends of my humanity.

THE GREAT WINTER WOOD PELLET RUSH OF '07

Dropped the broom in mid-sweep
grabbed my breakfast bowl
forgot all else
and left home

a rush of adrenalin
drawing me to the store
a fever kindled in the instant of that call
"Come for those bags, while they last!"

Dashing in,
wondering how many
dare I ask for? Six, ten?

Paid for the goods
precious seconds ticking by,
cars revving in the yard
lined up for that last palette.

"Five bags apiece!"
quieted all questions
the hurried, satisfying thumps
landing in the back of the truck.

Driving away with the catch,
feeling triumphant
in taking so much.

Perhaps, the price is higher
than the tallest pines
lower than the earth's fiery bowels
wider than our appetites
as slender as the bonds
that bind us here.

And what if that same fever,
that same unfulfillable need,
were to grip and drive me
to the heaped palettes of truths
sitting unsold
in my own backyard?

HEAV'N

I dreamed that you were no longer judging
me on my heart's murmurings
but on how well I'd cleaned the fridge-freezer —
not just the outer doors or the salad compartments
but both sides of the grungy, smeared stained
glass, and all the dark nooks and crannies
where I'd stored assorted batteries, egg dyes,
cat antibiotic, and cloning gel for profuse rooting

and on how I'd cleaned the kitchen cooker —
not just the rings and trays, or even the oven
racks and sides and around the wires leading
to the light that no longer works; but
also whether I'd scraped and chiseled
the congealed blackened spills
mounting under the top.

And when you'd inspected them from top
to bottom, I saw you placing everyone in cells,
apartments, condos, and grand houses
according to their station and destination.
Looking at me, you scratched your head
and shuffled me off to a large stable
where thousands gathered in all conditions,
heaving and lowing, braying and bleating
crowing, singing, and grazing.

On waking, I felt cold steel bars
and the fading barn reeked of heaven.

DEATH'S FISHER

Black feet
   stately glide
      small ripples
         barely sound.

      Bead-like eye
      leads softly
      snaking nape
    each footfall
    yielding greater sight.

Black foot
   stately glides
     slender white
     coiled neck

    tightly sprung
   stab's release
  quicksilvery glint
 twirls in
stunning beak.

    Rapid toss
      pulsing gullet
        one-way descent.
      Black feet
     stately glide.

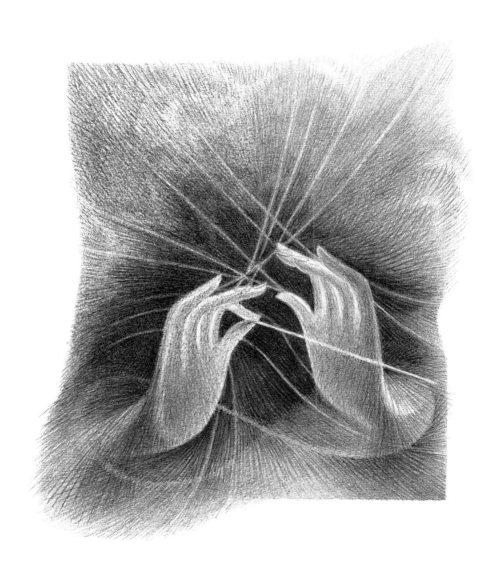

THE CONDUCTOR

—*Inspired by Jeffrey Kahane's deep humanity*

As his hands
    bring down, with sweat
        and attentiveness

that which is poised
    waiting to be plucked
        from the inaudible

and invisible,
    intertwined with the lattice
        of our receptivity

into a supple sound tapestry —
    so seam
        weavers of matter.

And are we not
    then
        all weavers?

Enmeshed

Look at that web almost burying the plant and the pot!
How on earth did it get there?
It's straddling the pointed tips of our succulent.
   Your tea's getting cold.
And it's cradling some of the dead 'uns.
   Yes.
And have you noticed how the color,
deep green in its center,
changes all the way to orange
and yellow at the edges
where the tiniest maroon thorns stick out?
   Hmmm.
You know, it looks a bit like an onion bulb.
   Well, I'm reading about global warming.
Do you think it hears the birdsong?
   Why not?
What about those trapped dead shoots, old flower-head,
and veined insect wings locked in its strands?
   Hmmm.
There's no spider in sight and no visible prey.
It's like an intricate structure, abandoned by its creator.
   Well, did you know the North Pole's shifting
   quarter of a mile every single day!
Oh!
Right by the pot's edge is a new green shoot. Must be its
offspring!
   Hmmm.

I wonder if *it* hears the trilling, feels wet drops, sun's ray
in a new way?

There are an awful lot of very concerned people.
See these older, wizened leaves peering over the edge.
Perhaps, they remember what lies beyond?

THE HOME

Heart thumping,
his reptilian bones
soak up the heat
as he readies for
the journey.

Rising up, up
on shaky legs
he shuffles;
slippered feet trail
across the chasm floor
like fleeting summer clouds.

Haltingly,
he hears his breath
creaking and whistling
through his lungs.

Limbs clenched
he reaches
the threshold
turns by degrees.

Backing
he grasps the rests,
lowers himself

with a dull thud
onto the seat.

Through panting.
parched lips outpour
"Kids're long gone.

Thank you Lord
for keeping me
one more day —
        one more day —
                away from that home."

OTHER THAN HERE

Most of my life
I'm drawn to places
other than here.

Of course, in hungry youth
I needed to travel
there.

Throughout adulthood
my thoughts and desires propel
into the stratospheres
or am I led
by an invisible noose?

Affects fling me into
fierce mountain passes
battling tribes
precipitous chasms.

Memories magnetically
sway me towards fading
frayed flowers.

Occasionally I visit *here*
when stunned by
a sudden scent, sound
or a look —

when my emotions sputter
into tears and between
the cracks of defeat
and relief
fresh vistas appear —

when feelings zing
at the amazing beings
planted about an
unblinkered view.

But how long
can I bear
to touch *here*
smell *here*
re-find *here*
before drifting off anew?

DAFFODILS

When those sunlings burst
out each year I say, "I will
plant more next season." And
sometimes I do and mostly I don't
but there are a few
gladdening hearts in the garden.

A vine given by a friend
has taken years
to yield small, sweet
yellowy-green grapes.

The calla lilies, too,
have been slow in expanding,
one or two garnered here and there
reclaimed from a neighbor's waste.

And what if I did sow mounds
and a spurting splash
blinded the eye —
would I be any the happier

when a single flowering —
then withering —
spurs with such force?

Closed Agenda

What if your Beloved said to you
"You are only as close to me
as you are to that cat!"
and you admired her,
from a distance,
petted and fed her,
heard her battering and scratching
the screen door for admittance in the night.

Could even convince yourself
you liked her but
would you truly miss her?
(Well, you do suffer from allergies!)
At times thought, "Isn't she sweet!"
but hated her bringing in bloody
gopher carcasses almost daily.

And you knew you'd continue
to go through the motions
unless a door slammed shut
or opened, or a voice inside cried
"Does she really ask for so much?"
Finally you see her
curled blissfully fetal
crumpling your agenda.

YOUR MAJESTY
— *After A Horse Frightened by a Lion, (1770)*
   by George Stubbs

Deep rumbling roar
earth tremors
blazing eyes
gaping jaw
closer   closer

within a leap —
petrified spine
hair on nape erect
prone I stay.

Waking I feel shame.
Was it cowardice?
Did I miss the king?

And so
this muscled
pale white stallion
cowering tail between
frozen non-rearing legs

mane screaming about
that mighty neck
locks flying
ears prostrate.

Glazed eye
mute nostril
limp dried lip
body bowed before
majesty.

How do you meet
your power, *your* fate?

Soft Flickerings

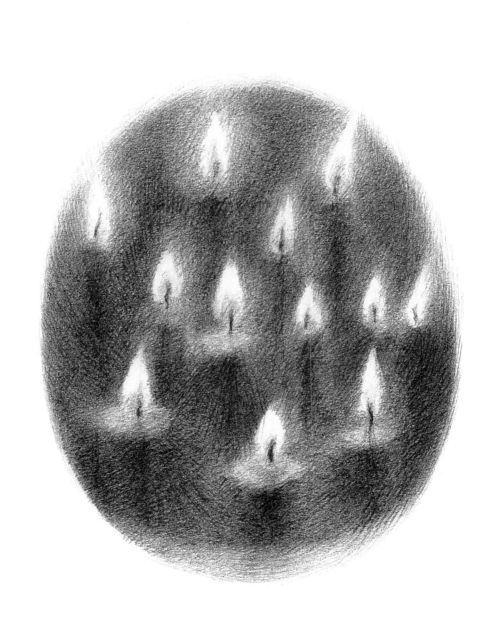

NEW YEAR

Our celebrations were small affairs
with one or two present at most,
like the welcome my wife and daughter
gave the New Year, with carefully
prepared round, sand-filled trays,
candles of all shapes and heights arranged
until the moment ignited and light
generously swirled and flowed
out and in our eyes
linked in wonder.

Or the birthdays of simple homemade
stirrings of cakes, smiles, and wings.

Now they fill my dark nights
with soft flickerings.

THE KISS

What if your
whiteness were
to shrivel to
brown

and your inner core
host of so many
insect friends
begins to change
into large green
interlinked cases
like a turtle
or a pineapple shell.

The top of
your yellow stamen
shrinks
to burning black
while your seed
pods swell
filling your body
with heavy fruit

until one day
your weight
bears you down
to the ground
where you lie
prostrate
with longing.

Your kernels
now yellow
turn into gold
and tunnel
the earth
so half-merged
you're waiting
for them
to soften and sag

letting
your pale seeds
slip out
of their amniotic sacs
and seal
the kiss.

BELLS

No bells ringing
no incense burning
no one but you.

No spoken sounds
no embracing arms
no one else but you.

Inner voices buzzing
deepening breathing
you're coming to you.

With or without stilling
something is flowing.

You're entering
a cavern resounding
of echoes beyond.

What will you bring
when you return?

Figments of darkness
bursts of light?

Or, perhaps
just you
hewed a little larger?

SOFT NIGHT

Soft night piercing screech
    the pair work the field

back and forth
    beat silent wings
        echo soft skirls

as one stands sentinel
    aloft the ridge
        high-pitched messages persist

flushing field mice, gophers, voles
    from peaceful nests —

Forswear your life
    to mightier intent they shrill
        until their prey is wrung.

WHEN I LOOK AT THE STARS

When I look at the stars
I hardly know their names —
the upturned W
a dragon's tail?

I just stare and stare
at their starriness —
countless worlds
scattered in bright patterns
and curves, emitting
stories that travel
light years to return
us to ourselves.

"Curious really!" I might have
told the cat beside me,
her marvelously arching back
and curling tail coiling and dipping,
or the crickets, their quiet ringing
under-and-overtones
constellating lunar rhythms,
or the twinkling airplane lights
rapidly gobbling night's canvas,
or the tingling chill on my cheeks
gnawing into bones, or
the sudden scuttle in the brush.
But I didn't.

I slipped them all
into my pocket
and brought them inside
to share with you.

Out of This World!

Fleshy, furry

strawberries wallow

peachy skins waft

nectarine yellow

small banana rounds sail

cosmic kindness

across a bowl of

stars ricochet, ricochet

far flung blueberry

overflowing milky whey

lazily among Galia melon

OUTFLANKED

Way before I clapped eyes on it,
my hand instinctively reached
for the flank of a beast rearing
through surging waves.

He was skinny, tired,
almost drowned, yet unbowed.
"I have long suffered your neglect.
Now, at last, you begin to feel me.

Climb up, climb up!
Astride my back
you'll gallop like the wind.
Together we'll take off!"

Sensing me hesitate, he growled
"Just mount. I will do the rest —
for I am stamping my feet
in the ground of your being."

THIS ACHE

For you
   my ache's antennae
      are constantly combing
         monitoring, marking.

For you
   my ache's flutterings
      fibrillate in
         sinuous waves.

For you
   my ache is a condor
      without prey
         endlessly scanning
           scarred horizons.

For you
   this ache is afire —
      knows no bounds —
         leaps canyons
           lights on sharp crags
      outer shells crack
   under red hot
marbled waves.

For you
   my ache pours
      blood-thick tears.

ODE TO MY MOTHER

You fought as a woman in a man's land whose tongue you barely spoke.

An artist at heart, between husband and kids, you painted, potted and drew. Your need to draw lessons from everything drove me nuts when I was young yet I, too, became a teacher.

So much of you is carved inside me — seeds of beauty, seeds of darkness, all longing for light and rest and peace, even those that never made it.

You crossed the Mediterranean alone with your two young boys to see the Acropolis and Pompeii, telling us to play on deck while you, though miserably sea-sick, kept a watchful eye, helping us off a small boat in Limassol. Locked out of a hotel room in France, you enticed a slender porter to crawl through a narrow window, until we heard a triumphant,

"*Voila!*"

For years you anguished over your youngest, whose wings were clipped by schizophrenia — how you would move heaven and earth to help him were it in your power to do so — and you did.

Your roundful laugh at your husband's oft repeated jokes, your fiery indignation when 'righting a wrong', your steadfast rule of kitchen and home, all dwarf my niggling annoyances at being so close to you.

I swore that I would never be like you, and I wasn't, and I am.

FALLEN FRUIT

I have fallen in love again;
I know this because I find myself
resting in a patch on the fallen
cracked trunk, old, rounded and open
and following you over the bank
as you slowly sweep across the field.

A cat's mew from her den
away in the blackberry bushes
follows me, as she beds herself
on a mole hill or hayed furrow,
rolls over into a "You know
what I want you to do" position

slants her closed eyes
earthy purring pumping limbs
stretching twice as long
as the day, blisses out
while I scratch her favorite spots.

Pausing under a tree,
picking and sniffing
through the Gravensteins,
yellow skins splashed with magenta
drip, firm formfuls of breathtaking

smells, a dull thud draws me
to the next. Stooping
to pick the prize, darkened
reds on pale yellow ground —
the promise of a rough crunchy taste

a branch stays my shirt.
Caught by the crook of the neck!
First I struggle, then
break into a chuckle,
"It's you I want —
snag me over and over again!"

THE COCKEREL'S CALL

I place my face against
    your smooth, wet trunk
        and plant a kiss
my body resting in you
    listening to sweet water
       symphonies.

Clear droplets
    hammock and sloop
       along your limbs
slowly gaining roundness
    weight, momentum
       then release.

A furry tongue deftly
    licks curled leafy tips.
       "Ee, ee, ee–ee–ee–e!
Ee, ee, ee–ee–ee–e!"
    scoops into
       morning's mountain
barely ruffling
    a bottomless bag
       of grain.

WHEN A CHILL SEA WIND

WHEN A CHILL SEA WIND

When a chill sea wind swirls in and starts to flirt
with reddening leaves, gusting streams of dusty earth
and berries droop and sour —
apronfuls of apple sunset skirts

soften and brown, insect friends abound
buzzing busily one final fling around the sugared vine
while hosts of unacknowledged spirits weave
greens into kindred rainbow colors.

As if from nowhere, speeding clouds spring
and sweep across the sun's face, now wanly lit —
small birds magnetically bestir, circle tightly
loudly summoning for lengthy flight.

The poplar and eucalyptus bow and bend
their frizzled clumps, bunched brown heads
of Queen Anne's lace fill to the brim with seed
and we, like early September pumpkins, are rushed

and boxed in the stores. Then perhaps the signs
point to a time of seeded contemplation.
One fresh-fallen leaf held up to the light
casts a spell breaking my day's petty betrayals

reflects a tree whose branches and branchlets
spread a filigree beyond all golden wealth.

BEACHED

Thick tubes with cone-like rubbery ends,
swollen amber sacs, dark serrated leaves,
smooth purples, stringy browns,
briny stench, frazzled strands
snake in and out
wrapped up in themselves —
a complex mass, a glorious mix
of convoluted tales.

Some harshly broken,
many leading down aisles
we would never wish to return;
some salty and bitter
run rough under our fingers,
some smoothed in the manifold retelling,
some still slippery and fresh
or creepy, irresistibly
drawing us into their tentacles
or grating like a rasp
with sharp rippling ridges
or slimy as jelly, attracting
swarming flies to a putrid feast.

These tangled masses —
like stranded whales —
wait for the turning tide
to take, swill, sway, rock,
caress and unravel us.

NETS

"There!"
The nurse slips the IV into the vein.
I gaze at the network on the back of my hand.
It stands out so clearly and flows into the filigree
net of brown winter vine crawling up the freeway
overpass columns, now dormant, stretching in a
hundred thousand tiny branchlets, with no hint
of summer's bushy carpet, to the carved
estero channels at low tide, silted
matrix for herons, egrets, mussels, oysters, clams —
spreading out with the flat flowing manta
rays beyond the laced play on the full moon's face
scanning your eyes, your veined
eyeballs, for fleeting emotions, until the
warmth of your gritty voice gently orders
"Just hold me, Honey, just hold me!"

ONLOOKER

I was just a passerby —
Never really looked or saw
the thin-ribbed critter
on the far side of the muddy field
until my daughter took me
into *his* arena.

Slowly we get to know each other.
I curry his coat —
the way she showed me —
firm, gentle, round curves
over ribs and rilles
and mounds of muscle

my fingers following his skin
brushing in long, smooth strokes
noting changes
in his hair's direction,
ovoid belly, hinged runner's legs.

As he guzzles his favorite grain
lips and tongue rhythmically churning
it into a bluish mush,
I clean out the water tank
then take my leave
with alfalfa treats.

Now he whinnies softly
at my approach. My young one
often sees what I don't —
a neglected four-legged living
on bare pasture with buckets
of love.

KALI'S COIN

The Berlin Wall loomed large
while a child in London
its numinosity
haunting my dreams
with tales of families
fleeing from East to West
sometimes miraculously making it
more often impaled in the attempt —
East Berlin depicted as a desert
of fear-filled conformity —
while West Berlin
a wild Harlem flowing with
Milk and Honey!
"When the Wall came tumblin' down"
swept by a freedom tsunami
shock waves ricocheted around the world
akin to the Twin Towers —
the flip side of Kali's coin —
her belt of a thousand swinging skulls
chiming with each step she dances
stamping or erasing
our embraced illusions.

WHEN I WAS YOUNG AND PROUD

When I was young and proud
   owner of a lawn
      it would have caused offense.
But now, singing dandelions
   innocently declare summer's height
      while couched between
thrive purple petaled lights —
   morning glory untouched
      by the whirring blade of notions
for Queen Anne's lace
   and soft bare feet
      to sink and rise
with violet-green swallows'
      first chirruping flights.

JUST WHEN YOU THINK IT'S OVER

Just when you think it's over —
that there's nothing more —
that you've dealt with it

your body raises a ruckus
kicking and screaming
you're killing me!

And those unwanted children
and grandchildren, run amok
tipping acid inside your guts.

Your mind taunts, how can you
act like such a baby!

While your millions of years
reply, all you need do is feel

not rid, resolve, sweep
under the rug, just
fully feel.

Finally, you're forced to admit
okay, there's room.

And in that room resounds
a long-exiled cry.

BUFFET

Gray, bespectacled, middle-aged,
light streaks of kindness
first drew us near,
kids and adults, and boy
there were plenty!

Snippets and snatches revealed
three children, two grown
the youngest adopted
mentally impaired —
elderly parents
in a nearby Home —
a husband
migraines, pains rarely shared.

"Haven't you got a lot on your plate?"
one day I suggested.
"Oh that," she chuckled wryly
"went years ago. First it
turned into a platter
then, a buffet."

CELEBRATION

slices of chatter
   cookies of laughter
      as bread, jam, and butter
   pass between

bubbles of thoughts
   glide and rise
      sips of smiles
   expand surprise

brush of lips and crumbs
   sparkling eyes
      touch of hands
   a wish —

the sweetness
      of This!

GROUND TO A PULP

Been stood on my feet for hours
washing dishes, cooking,
washing more dishes,
not counting the shopping
on the way home
and yes, I'm bound
to end the day —
washing dishes.

There's only the two of us
yet plates and cups magically
sprout on counter-tops
tables, easy chairs.

Chores used to be something
to rush through a.s.a.p.
to more urgent things,
like movies, e-mail, u-name-its.

Now, while slowly wading
through tiredness and water
I settle.
Child's absorbed in homework
cat's content.
This is a good task.
I am doing well
to serve the moment.
What's more important?

A Sweep of Galaxies

So different was this shore
    after winter's beatings —
        so different.

Sandbanks collapsed
    washed away, re-stacked,
wooden walkways crumpled,
    upended trunks tossed like straws.

The waves race in
    following their own rhyme
etching, erasing
    doubled folds of time.

Each wet step
    slides into a pool
of liquid glass
    as thousands of particles awake

rapidly whirling into a vortex
    surging, merging in ocean's lap,
trailing long white
    frothing gene-strings.

A sweep of galaxies
   a moment's trace
      a dance of three-toed feet
         a damp imprint
            fluttering of wings.

EARTH DANCES

SPRING

With a whoop and a fling
blossoms she brings
singing, it's April
it's April, it's April.

Pop out to see
my purple tablecloth billow
waves of songbird
on branches and twigs
pink and white bursts.

Step lively to
fall's rattling shells
crows' flap 'n gab
buzzing wings and legs.

Under the gliding moon
owls beat the meadow
blazing with thirst
eight silken eyes sip
my million morning pearls.

MUTE MILLENNIAL

We gape at
the Wall
the mall
tall towers
twin flowers
deserted lots
hot spots
fantasy lovers.

Alone, eyes inward
her writhing
belly ripples —
feet braced
teeth on edge
gasping furnace red
beads of sweat pour —
contraction after contraction
grip her throat.

We goggle at
the war
the pall
heroes
faces

stained spots
neighbors
hoped-for saviors.

‖: Alone, eyes inward
her writhing
belly ripples.
Waves of groans
circle her globe.:‖

WIRED

First She had to heave up mountains,
then cool her blood with ice and wait
a little while for rock to tumble
shatter, allow her glacier plow
to rake the valleys out, until
the last few seconds, so they say,
we came and settled, built dry walls
up to the crags, scattered sheep to eat
forest shoots, and so came pasture.

And still her brooks course through
her veins, lilting and sighing and
spinning their ways into lake and sea
as she tilts quietly
ominous, egg-timer wired
to our words, feelings, thoughts —
weighing whether to flip it over
or, like the show with too small
an audience, simply close the stage.

WAS IT WRIT?

Was it writ that first
she set her winds to whistle
spiraling round, bringing all weathers;
second, through mist, fog and fern
sortied the soft whistling owl;
third, shepherd intoned to his sharp-eared friend
fetching the lost from bog and fen;
fourth, thundered our jets;
fifth, deafening silence?
Sixth, ructions and ripples convulse!

Or might we
funnel absolute energies —
swiveling like a deer's ears
towards the source of sounds?

Furies calm;
quakes subside;
walls of hate crack.
We laugh at our pettiness.
A never-before-dance
begins to spin.

EMBRACE

Chest pressed against its strand-like trunk, arms loosely wrapped around its matted bark, his being rapidly whirled, an elevator dropping twenty floors or the steepest water slide descent — without jolt, just a sensation of soft flames — eddying reeds in a river set against a moonless night. He could not tell whether these flames or sinews were those of the tree bringing him in or of his own fibrous being. They continued flowing, fading as the darkness deepened, not quite pitch, an undying pool. It lasted a few, untallied moments before he allowed his arms to drop, stepped back, and with a bow took leave, his body marked with an invisible imprint. This was simple to step into, like a pair of well-loved shoes left lying untouched about the house.

Old and Delved

Dappling, flaking, silvery brown,
cracked, pecked, holy, cleft trunk,
limbs hanging by a thread.

Thicket of an old, unpruned apple tree,
rich, leafy mold stewing
in your mossy base —
home to thousands.

One hundred years
of hollowing
to bear everything —
sweet fruit.

One hundred years
of hollowing
to bear everything —
sweet fruit!

THE INVERNESS RIDGE FIRE

Fifteen years ago this fall, fire swept along the ridge. All night I watched cackling flames leap wildly from hill to hill, as people's homes, intruding on pine clad slopes, succumbed quickly to its red hot breath.

Thousands of hands attempted to staunch this fierce fertility rite, a cyclical outpouring ejecting billions of seeds into soft, blackened folds. Sounds of choppers warned of war as they dropped and scooped from the bay, discharging their watery cargo at the front.

Under a dawning sun, I stood at its flaming edge, heat blasting up from the valley prickling and tingling my skin. Bishop pines hurled searing balls of sap, like slingshots or missiles, whistling to their kin, who in turn, joined the furnacing procession. On that brink, in that moment, the pungency and crushing roar, mesmerized corneas, superheated senses, ignited my heart, as ardent tongues licked at my feet, hissing, "Why resist?"

Along the bay, little remains of the charred skyline — tall green offspring bear new witness. While picking huckleberries on its hillsides, enjoying their gentle-breasted descent, or nestling my face in honeysuckle, I sometimes glimpse hers, unveiled, leaping along the ridge, hair wildly streaming where she wills.

Moth Behemoth

Cecropia behemoth
lying in the road
your fine feather-like antennae
and massive wings
spanning east to west

furry brown body
upon stout brown legs —
undercarriage to a glory
of painted panels.

Here, Seminole and Algonquin
in wood and bead
found delicacy of line
subtle color fusion

the Navajo Nation
stunningly intricate
dyed design

Pomo, Miwok
painstakingly wrought
bighearted basketry

Acoma
sacred, secret
dazzling-patterned clay.

Let me lift you
on a leaf
for our coming journey.

Your rare magnificence
is fanning out, fanning out —
lightening a way.

BETWEEN THE TWO SHORES

Cloud shadows sweep   underfoot
whisking sand streamers   snake low
yet   this is no desert

waves continuously   conceive
         along the shore
gulls, sanderlings
         eye each crest's retreat
plucking mollusks   in razor beaks.

Around the curved walls
         of the estero's womb
seals softly bark
         brown pelicans rise and dive
spreadeagled wings   glide
         just a few feet
to fish for catch
         we cannot see
this is   Eden's garden
         we are in its play —
why do I visit
         so infrequently?

And Earth Spoke

Pray, pray for forgiveness,
and ask before you act. Wait —
wait for my answer.
Only then can I subtract
what is necessary for Life —
your life — to continue
to grow.

Songs

WHEN I LOOK AT THE STARS

words: Raphael Block
music: Sarah Saulsbury

This is an extract from the score. For more information contact the author.

Unbreakable Peace

Raphael Block

SPRING INTO STILLNESS

1

Raphael Block

I'm sped on a use-less spree,_____ when I don't spring in - to still-ness— all o - ver the map,_____ ex-cept where I need to be. So, I knock and en-ter the cham - ber where my mind's mach-in - a - tions stop and clear. Fresh rain-drops,_____ fresh, round rain-drops,_____ fresh rain-drops_____ sloop and_____ spill when_____ I vis-it the gar - den. I'm loose on a may-hem trail_____ _____ when I won't swing in - to still-ness— run - ning_____ rings_____ all a-round my - self. So, I cross the bor - der,_____ duck through_____ tan-gled_____ trees till my feet find a peb-bled_____ path_____ weav - ing through the maze.

2

Magic is Here

Moderato

1

Raphael Block

Can you touch____ the point of still - ness____ just be -

fore____ birds take off?____ Could you reach____ through dark-'ning

leaves____ to a fie - ry win-ter glow?____ Would you

dare crawl un - der the bel - ly of a Cor - gi wad-dling home?____

____ Would you dare crawl un - der the bel - ly of a

Cor - gi wad-dling home?____ I

leaped in____ to the fox-'s mouth— it snapped shut____ as the birds took

Hanging by a Thread

Raphael Block

1. I Saw an X - ray to-day.____ It showed me clear - ly hanging by a thread. What's it made of, you might say—____ I asked___ the den - i-zens of love.____

2 Is it made of copper or gold,
silver, sapphire, amethyst?
The four winds whistled
the four winds shook—
it's not made of what you think.

3 Is it made of cedar or pine,
rosewood, elm or redwood?
The forests shivered
the forests cried—
it cannot be carved or sliced.

4 Is it made of must or myrrh,
eucalyptus, wild pepprmint?
The meadows banked,
the meadows swayed—
its essence can't be drunk or smelled.

5 Is it made of tears or smiles
like an acrobat or a clown?
The circus tent billowed
the tightrope twanged—
it's not made of tricks or masks.

6 Ia it made of arrogance
anger, envy or regret?
The moon bent low
to whisper in my ear—
it's not made of what you fear.

7 Is it made of purple hues
lavendar or coral blues?
The seven seas hollered,
the seven seas rolled—
it's the color of water, so we've been told.

8 Is it found in the ocean deep
or in the reaches of cosmic space?
The stars laughed
the stars shim-shimmered
just tap the stillness in your treasure chest—

tap____ the still - ness____ in your trea - sure's chest—___ just

tap____ the still - ness____ in your trea - sure chest.____

ABOUT THE AUTHOR

Born on a kibbutz in Israel to pioneering parents, Raphael Block spent his boyhood playing on the hills of Haifa.

Just before turning nine, his family returned to London. Learning English shaped his ear for sounds, and the British climate and temperament fashioned his life over the next 25 years, until he met and married an American living in London.

In 1993 they moved to Northern California with their daughter. His partner died from cancer in 2002, and for the following years he feels it was his privilege to raise their child.

Raphael has worked with children of all ages for almost 30 years. A long time meditator, he breathes in wonder at the earth's and our own rhythmic ebb and flow. He dwells in an old apple orchard outside of Sebastopol, and is often accompanied by musicians when performing.

Raphael suffers with Chron's Disease. He says of this, "It has been a great teacher, forcing me over the years to pay attention to messages from my gut and relate to my emotions in a fuller and more conscious way. In 2008, after surgery, Chron's swept into the forefront of my life. Not only did I have to retire, but much more difficult has been the process of learning to lovingly care for myself. Leading life at a much slower pace is great for observing, writing, and being. The daily opportunities for gratitude and amazement seem to multiply with a life-threatening illness."

PRESS PRODUCERS

FRIEND OF THE PRESS
- HEARTFELT THANKS

Anatoly Molotkov
Beverly Riverwood
Lilith Rogers

S. Preston Chase
Joan Michelson
Anonymous

SUPPORTER OF THE PRESS
- DEEPEST GRATITUDE

Judith Tucker
Linda Milks
Rebecca Hubbard
Magick
Diana Badger
Miles Peterson
Susan Dullack
Mary Eisenhauer
Lillian Madera Schuller

Michael Milosch
Zachary Ritter
Maria Rosales
Patricia Kelly
Jean Wong
Linda McGonigal
Katelin Holloway & Ben
Ramirez
Anonymous

SPONSOR OF THE PRESS
- PROFOUND APPRECIATION

J. Glenn & Barbara Evans
Joyce Downs
Nicole Woo
Sylvia Levinson
Tricia Ferguson
Edward Maupin

Clare & Jon Allen
Sharon Bard
Kelly Gazaway
Cynthia Albers
Ailbe O'Brien
Anonymous

PATRON OF THE PRESS
- KEEN AFFECTION

Paul Dolinsky
Tomas Gayton
Carina Wagner
Peggy Gregory
Albert G. Jordan

Sandra Stillwell
Chris Hoffman
Joseph Milosch
The Entrekin Foundation
Anonymous

PRESS PRODUCERS

I would like to thank all of those who worked on, and participated in, our *Summer 2013 Season of Poetry* campaign to raise finances for this and two other volumes of poetry. Thanks to James Downs, Devon Peterson, Joyce Downs, and Dan Davis. Also, thanks to the three poets: Lyn Lifshin, Raphael Block and Joseph Milosch. And, of course, thanks to all of these people who contributed so generously to this effort. Small poetry press publishing is a joy to do but certainly costs money and these Producers, as in any artistic effort, are the ones who make it possible.

Thank you!

— John Peterson, Publisher

Lightning Source UK Ltd.
Milton Keynes UK
UKOW03f0805240314

228697UK00002B/35/P